D1367254

American

JAZZ

BESSIE
SMITH

KATHLEEN TRACY

Mitchell Lane
PUBLISHERS

P.O. Box 196
Hockessin, Delaware 19707

American JAZZ

Benny Goodman

Bessie Smith

Billie Holiday

Charlie Parker

Count Basie

Dizzy Gillespie

Louis Armstrong

Miles Davis

Ornette Coleman

Scott Joplin

Printing   1   2   3   4   5   6   7   8   9

Library of Congress Cataloging-in-Publication Data

Tracy, Kathleen.
  Bessie Smith / by Kathleen Tracy.
     p. cm. — (American jazz)
  Includes bibliographical references and index.
  ISBN 978-1-61228-271-8 (library bound)
  1. Smith, Bessie, 1894–1937—Juvenile literature.
  2. Singers—United States—Biography—Juvenile literature. I. Title.
  ML3930.S67T73 2013
  782.421643092—dc23
  [B]
                                           2012008589

eBook ISBN: 9781612283470

                                                    PLB

Contents

Chapter 1

Klan Encounter

On a sultry July night in 1927, singer Bessie Smith was preparing to give a concert under a tent in Concord, North Carolina. At the time, Bessie was one of the most famous blues performers in the United States. Concord was one of several stops on her music tour. While many Southerners, both black and white, came to enjoy her show, some Southerners resented Bessie's success because she was African American. Even though the Civil War had been over for more than sixty years, race relations in the South were often tense. Tonight, that tension would flare, and Bessie would face one of the most fearsome groups of Southerners to organize against black Americans: the Ku Klux Klan.

In the years following the Civil War, most former slaves chose to stay in the South. During this time, called Reconstruction, laws were passed to protect African Americans' civil rights, and they enjoyed their newfound freedom. Teachers from the North came to the South to teach both young and older African Americans how to read and write. Blacks moved from the country to cities in search of better wages and housing. Although blacks and whites lived side by side, the races tended not to mix socially.

For the white majority, still bruised by losing the war and having to adjust their way of life, the changes brought by Reconstruction were way too much, way too soon. Even though the law saw African Americans as citizens, many of these whites felt they were better than the people who had been slaves. The Ku Klux Klan wanted to maintain this idea of white supremacy.

The first branch of the Ku Klux Klan was formed in Pulaski, Tennessee, in 1866. Over the years more branches were established throughout the South. Many Klan leaders had been members of the Confederate Army. At first, the group's goal was to keep blacks from using their newly gained rights as citizens, including the right to vote. But soon the group became a terrorist organization, using violence to achieve their goal. Klansmen wearing white robes, pointed cardboard hats, and masks tortured and killed many African Americans. They also killed whites who supported blacks, even performers.

Although the Klan's actions were illegal, many Southerners agreed with their ideas of white supremacy. They did not stop anyone who tried to keep blacks "in their place." In fact, many southern states and towns passed laws designed to limit the civil rights that were granted to African Americans under Reconstruction. Much to the surprise of many northerners, the U.S. Supreme Court upheld these laws. In one ruling, the Court overturned the Civil Rights Act of 1875 as unconstitutional. In another, it ruled that states were allowed to pass laws that kept services, facilities, and public accommodations such as hotels separated by race. After that ruling, Southern legislatures passed a flurry of anti–African American segregation laws. These became known as the Jim Crow laws.

Even though they were no longer slaves, African Americans were treated like second-class citizens. Schools, hospitals, restaurants, and even public parks could legally be designated as whites only areas. In several states, it was illegal for an African American to marry a white person. It was also against the law in some cities for African Americans to be out late at night.

The Klan disbanded around 1869, after too many criminals had joined the group and prominent citizens, such as judges and lawmen, dropped out. But in 1915, a three-hour-long silent movie helped revive the movement. Called *Birth of a Nation,* the movie was based on a 1905 novel by Thomas F. Dixon called *The Clansman: An Historical Romance of the Ku Klux Klan.* The book looked at Reconstruction from a Southern viewpoint.

In *Birth of a Nation,* African Americans are depicted as the cause of all social, political, and economic problems in the post–Civil War South. The Ku Klux Klan is painted as The Savior of Southern people. While the movie sparked race riots in the North, Dixon and the filmmaker, D.W. Griffith, stood behind their message. "My object is to teach the North, the young North, what it has never known—the awful suffering of the white man during the dreadful Reconstruction period," Dixon said.[1]

The National Association for the Advancement of Colored People (NAACP) protested the movie. They denounced it as racist, but efforts to boycott the film largely failed. Later, the group claimed that the popularity of *The Birth of a Nation* was responsible for the revival of the Ku Klux Klan in the 1920s.

By that time, the majority of African Americans in the South lived in poverty. To survive, they learned to live with segregation. For the most part, they kept a low profile and did not cause trouble. Causing trouble drew attention, which could be deadly, especially with the Klan lurking.

Bessie Smith had never been one to keep a low profile—quite the contrary. Bessie was known for her temper and wasn't shy about expressing herself. She proudly embraced her race and heritage. When a group of Klansmen surrounded her performance tent dressed in their robes and masks, she wasn't afraid. And when they threatened to disrupt her concert by collapsing the tent and trapping her and the audience inside, she was irate.

She asked some of the stagehands to get rid of the Klansmen, but they refused. They were terrified to face the masked men in pointed hats directly. According to author Chris Albertson, Bessie went outside and confronted the Klan, asking, "What [do] you think you're doing?"

Bessie shook her fist at the intruders and told them to leave. "I'll get the [entire] tent out here if I have to," she yelled. "You just pick up them sheets and run!"[2]

Not used to meeting any sort of resistance, the Klansmen stared at Bessie, shocked. Knowing they'd be outnumbered if Bessie made good

Directed by D. W. Griffith, *The Birth of a Nation* was based on *The Clansman,* a novel set in the post-Civil War south. Critics accused the movie of promoting prejudice with its sympathetic depiction of the Ku Klux Klan.

on her threat to involve the audience, the men left. Bessie kept swearing at them until they disappeared into the humid night, then went back inside the tent and calmly continued her performance.

While Bessie refused to be intimidated and managed to carve out a successful career in spite of the obstacles faced by African Americans in the early twentieth century, she was not immune to the effects of racism. Many people believe the politics of segregation in the end may have cost Bessie Smith her life.

The NAACP

Based in Baltimore, Maryland, the National Association for the Advancement of Colored People, known as the NAACP, is the oldest civil rights organization in the United States. It was formed to protect and promote the civil rights of black Americans. The organization continues to fight racism through political activism and education programs.

The NAACP was established on February 12, 1909. At that time race relations in America were very tense, especially in the South. The horrific practice of lynching, where white men murdered blacks by hanging them from trees, was commonplace. In 1908, there had been a violent race riot in Springfield, Illinois—the same city where Abraham Lincoln is buried.

Appalled by the increasing violence against blacks, a group of white social liberals arranged a meeting to discuss racial injustice. The result was the formation of the NAACP, on the 100th anniversary of Lincoln's birthday.

Since its formation, the NAACP has led the fight against racism. They were a primary supporter of a federal law against lynching and other race-based hate crimes. During the Depression, which was particularly disastrous for blacks, the organization started focusing on employment equality. And during the 1950s and 1960s the NAACP worked with leaders such as Martin Luther King, Jr. to help pass the historic Civil Rights Act of 1964.

Even though race relations have gotten better, there is still prejudice. So the NAACP remains a vocal advocate for equality of all kinds—political, economic, medical, and social.

Chapter **2**

Born to Perform

Like many Southern states, Tennessee has a troubled history when it comes to race relations. It supplied more Confederate soldiers than any other state and is where the Ku Klux Klan was founded. Tennessee was also the first state to pass a Jim Crow law: in 1881, it voted to segregate train cars.

Just three years later, on April 15, 1894, Bessie Smith was born in Chattanooga, Tennessee. She was the youngest of seven children. The family was poor, and lived in a one-room cabin. Bessie's father William, a Baptist minister, died not long after Bessie was born. By the time she was nine years old, she had also lost her mother, Laura, along with two brothers. Her oldest sister, Viola, became head of the family and moved her younger siblings to a tenement apartment.

Viola ran a small laundry business to support her brothers and sisters, cleaning clothes by boiling water in large containers on an outdoor coal stove. Bessie and her brother Andrew raised extra money for the family by performing on Chattanooga street corners. Bessie would sing and dance, and Andrew would play the guitar. Even as a young girl, Bessie had a distinctive, powerful voice that captivated passersby. Viola did not really approve, but the nickels and dimes Bessie brought home helped feed and clothe the family.

In 1904, Bessie's brother Clarence joined the Moses Stokes' Traveling Show, a touring minstrel and vaudeville company. He worked as a comedian and dancer. Encouraged by her brother, Bessie also started performing with a number of traveling shows. These companies toured around 40 weeks of the year, with each tour called a season.

Vaudeville theaters during Bessie's time tended to be segregated—some theaters catered to white audiences and others catered to black audiences. Ironically, most of the black theaters were owned by white businessmen, although a few were owned by African Americans.

In the early days of vaudeville, performers would send newspaper clippings about their acts to the theater managers in hopes of getting a booking. By 1909, black vaudeville became organized into a formal circuit called the Theater Owners Booking Association (TOBA). This group determined which acts performed at what theaters, the length of their booking, and how much the performers were paid. TOBA started with 31 theaters and eventually grew to include around 100. But not all black theaters signed up with TOBA. Many of the more successful black theaters, such as those in Harlem (a district in New York City), remained independent.

In 1911, Bessie met Wayne "Buzzin" Burton at a theater in Birmingham, Alabama. The speed at which Burton could tap dance earned him his nickname. Beginning in 1912, Wayne and Bessie started performing as a duo. At the end of that performing season, they renamed their act Burton and Burton and joined the L.D. Joel Theater Companies in Atlanta,

By uniting black vaudeville theaters in 1909, TOBA reduced competition for performers. The result was that black performers in this circuit were paid less and had fewer choices for touring arrangements than their white counterparts.

which included the Joel, Dixie, and Central theaters. They performed together in many major cities, including Philadelphia, Chicago, St. Louis, and Washington, D.C. Despite gaining a following of fans, they ended their partnership.

Later, when Bessie was seventeen, Clarence arranged for her to audition for the Moses Stokes' Traveling Show. The company's managers were impressed and hired her as a dancer. Physically, Bessie was an imposing figure, standing nearly six feet tall with a full figure. But it was her voice that drew the most attention. She was moved to the chorus then quickly advanced to become one of the show's featured singers. In addition to her singing, Bessie engaged audiences with her humor and enjoyed interacting with people in the crowd. After just two years with the show, she was as popular as the company's star performer, Ma Rainey.

In the book *Jazz People,* guitarist Danny Barker remembers the singer's stage presence. "Bessie Smith was a fabulous deal to watch. She was a pretty large woman and . . . she dominated a stage. You didn't turn your head when she went on. You just watched Bessie. If you had any church background like people who came from the South as I did, you would recognize a similarity between what she was doing and what those preachers and evangelists from there did, and how they moved people . . . She could bring about mass hypnotism."[1]

In 1915 Bessie joined Rainey as a performer with Pat Chappelle's Rabbit's Foot Minstrels and then moved on to various other companies. Toward the end of the decade, Bessie had established her own Atlanta-based showcase called the Liberty Belles Revue. Even though vaudeville acts included doing skits and dancing, it was Bessie's singing that attracted audiences. By this time in America, blues music was becoming mainstream, and Bessie built her career on it.

The Mississippi Delta is considered the birthplace of the blues. Jazz and blues are considered the only true American music forms. Their roots can be found in the African spirituals sung by slaves while they worked in the fields. The songs expressed the hardships the slaves experienced. As the music evolved, the blues reflected the black experience in white-controlled America; it also dealt with overcoming life's general trials and tribulations. Over time, regional blues styles developed, such as Memphis blues in Tennessee and Delta blues around the mouth of the Mississippi.

After the Civil War ended, African-American men in the South did not have many job opportunities. They could work in the fields for extremely low wages or be traveling minstrels, performers who sang songs, recited poetry, and danced. Minstrels helped popularize the blues, which were a common part of their acts. For a long time blues songs were sung from memory, passed down orally through the years. One of the first documented blues songs to be written is W.C. Handy's "Memphis Blues," written in 1909.

As the music industry blossomed, blues songs were recorded, and the genre became more popular. Mother Nature also helped. Starting in 1913, southern cotton crops were pummeled by a series of devastating disasters. First, the global price of cotton fell, forcing some farmers, and their sharecroppers, out of business. Then an infestation of boll weevils wiped out crops.

It is believed the boll weevil first invaded America in 1892 through Brownsville, Texas, from its native Mexico. Within thirty years, the weevil had spread throughout all the eastern cotton-growing states, from Mississippi to Virginia—a rate of 55 miles a year. The speed at which the weevil spread caught many off-guard and buckled local economies. That, compounded by the severe floods of 1915 in the Mississippi Valley, prompted the start of what became known as the Great Migration, one of the largest relocations of citizens in United States history. Between 1915 and 1930, it is estimated that more than two million African Americans moved to northern industrial cities via the Mississippi River and the railroad. They took the blues with them to places such as St. Louis, Chicago, and Detroit.

Through her many years of touring, Bessie built a large, loyal fan base. People would stand in line for hours to buy tickets to her shows. But it was her recording contracts that would make Bessie Smith a household name and the greatest blues star of her time.

Ma Rainey

Ma Rainey was born Gertrude Pridgett on April 26, 1886, in Columbus, Georgia—although the 1900 Census lists her birth as September 1882. She began performing at The First African Baptist Church when she was about twelve years old. After she first heard blues music around 1902, she began mixing blues in with her performances.

Pridgett married singer and dancer William "Pa" Rainey on February 2, 1904. Her stage name became Madame Gertrude Rainey, and then simply Ma Rainey. She and Pa Rainey sang and danced in black minstrel shows, including the Rabbit's Foot Minstrels, where Ma met Bessie Smith. A rumor started that Ma kidnapped Bessie and made her join the minstrel show, but this story was later proven to be just that—a rumor.

Ma Rainey and her Georgia Jazz Band

In 1923, as recorded music was becoming more popular, Ma Rainey signed her first contract with Paramount Records. That year she released "Bad Luck Blues," "Bo-Weevil Blues," and "Moonshine Blues"—and then dozens more over the next few years. She became known as "the Mother of the Blues" and "Songbird of the South." TOBA booked her on a four-year tour, singing for the big bands of Tommy Dorsey and Fletcher Henderson.

In 1935, after the blues went into decline and she fulfilled her final recording contract, Rainey bought two theaters in Columbus, Georgia. She ran both the Lyric and the Airdrome until 1939, when she died from a heart attack. She is in both the Blues Foundation's Hall of Fame and the Rock and Roll Hall of Fame.

Chapter 3

Empress of the Blues

While her career is well documented, some aspects of Bessie Smith's personal life remain vague. For example, in 1920 Bessie married a man named Earl Love. Not much is known about how they met or what their life together was like. What is known is that Love died a year or two after they were married.

In 1921, Bessie moved to Philadelphia, where she auditioned for two record companies: Okeh Records and Harry Pace's Black Swan Records. Both labels opted not to sign her to a deal. Some music historians believe it was because Bessie was very dark skinned. Music historians report that lighter-skinned African Americans like Ethel Waters were generally given many more opportunities in show business. While Bessie may have been used to prejudice, she disliked the double standard and allegedly resented lighter-skinned blues singers, who in her eyes had it easier than she did.

Despite living in the North, Bessie did not mingle with white society the way some other African-American singers had. Whether Bessie chose not to or was never given the chance to is not known. By all accounts, Bessie could have a difficult personality off stage. She was moody, used vulgar language, and drank excessively. By her twenties, Bessie was an alcoholic.

In 1922, while performing at Horah's Cabaret in Philadelphia, Bessie met Jack Gee, a handsome security guard. On their first date, Gee—who also had a hot temper—got into a fight and ended up getting shot. He spent five weeks in the hospital. Bessie visited him every day, and when he was released, Bessie and Jack moved in together. They were married June 7, 1923, beginning what would prove to be a volatile, often violent relationship.

By this time, Bessie's recording career had taken off. Just a few years earlier, in 1920, Mamie Smith—who was not related to Bessie—made the first vocal blues record, "Crazy Blues." The record became a hit, selling 100,000 copies within a month of its release.

Prior to "Crazy Blues," music executives didn't think there was any money to be made by marketing to the black community. The success of the record changed their minds. Suddenly several record companies were rushing to make and release blues records, which were known as race records. Most of these recordings were marketed in the South and in areas of the North that had large black communities. Interestingly, in the South, the records were equally popular with whites.

Frank Walker, the head of Columbia's Race Records, invited Bessie to New York. Jack Gee pawned his watch and security guard uniform to buy Bessie a red dress to wear for her first recording session with Columbia. She arrived at the studio with her friend and pianist Clarence Williams on February 15, 1923. Bessie was so nervous, Walker sent Bessie home and rescheduled the session. Her first contract with Columbia paid Bessie $125 per releasable recording—equal to about $1,680 in 2012.

The next day Bessie recorded "Gulf Coast Blues" and "Down-hearted Blues," which sold a staggering 780,000 copies within

GULF COAST BLUES

By CLARENCE WILLIAMS

BESSIE SMITH

CLARENCE WILLIAMS

six months. Columbia Records signed Bessie to an eight-year contract, with a slight increase in pay per releasable recording. Bessie, however, did not receive any royalties. Between 1923 and 1931, Bessie would record 160 titles for Columbia and become one of their best-selling artists.

While she earned only a modest sum for her records, the publicity the recordings gave her helped her sell tour tickets. For live gigs, she earned a minimum of $1,500 a week. She bought a custom-designed railroad car to use when traveling to performances with her troupe. The car had two stories, a kitchen, a bathroom, and four bedrooms. Besides allowing her to travel with all the comforts of home, her car allowed her to avoid issues with Southern hotels that would not rent rooms to blacks.

Bessie also sent a lot of her earnings to Viola. She had also bought her sister a house in Philadelphia. But Bessie's generosity infuriated Jack, especially since he felt he should be in control of Bessie's money. As a result, there was constant tension between Jack and Bessie's family.

Things were not much better between Bessie and Jack. When she toured, she drank heavily, frequently got into physical fights, and had affairs. Sometimes she would also disappear for days at a time, usually to go on a drinking binge. Jack did not drink and did not like partying. He spied on Bessie and would get angry when he caught her misbehaving. Gee was often physically abusive. They broke up several times, only to get back together.

In 1925, while in Chattanooga for a show, Bessie got into a fight at an after-show party. A drunk guest made inappropriate advances toward one of her chorus girls, so Bessie punched him. When she left the party, the man confronted her outside and stabbed her in the side. Irate, Bessie ran after her attacker for a couple of blocks before collapsing. The wound was serious, but Bessie still performed the following night.

At the height of her popularity, Bessie made the equivalent of $20,000 per week in today's money. She became known for her flamboyant fashion style, both on- and off-stage.

In 1926, Bessie and Jack adopted a son they named Jack Jr. But having a child did not help the marriage, which remained combative. Later that year, while traveling in her railcar to a performance in Alabama, Bessie found out Jack was having a romantic relationship with one of her chorus girls. When Jack met the train at the station, Bessie pulled out a gun and shot at him. He avoided injury by running down the train tracks.

Performing provided a welcome escape for Bessie from her messy private life. As her records made her more popular, enthusiastic fans would greet her at tour stops. They loved her flamboyant image—she became known for her costumes, fringed shawls, colorful dresses, gaudy headdresses, and jeweled caps. Most of all, they loved her singing, which had earned her the nickname Empress of the Blues.

In the book *Early Jazz*, Günther Schuller analyzed Bessie's singing, saying she had "a remarkable ear for and control of intonation in all its subtlest functions; a perfectly centered, naturally produced voice (in her prime); an extreme sensitivity to word meaning and the sensory, almost physical, feeling of a word; and, related to this, superb diction and what singers call projection. She was certainly the first singer . . . to value diction, not for itself, but as a vehicle for conveying emotional states . . . Perhaps even more remarkable was her pitch control. She handled this with such ease and naturalness that one is apt to take it for granted. Bessie's fine microtonal shadings . . . are all part of a personal, masterful technique of great subtlety."[1]

Bessie continued to be a musical trailblazer. In 1925, her "Cake-Walking Babies" was the first electronically recorded song and the first time Bessie recorded using a microphone. She also recorded five songs for Columbia with Louis Armstrong, including W.C. Handy's "St. Louis Blues," considered by many to be one of the best blues recordings ever.

As the 1920s wound down, Bessie was on top of the blues world. She was the highest-paid black entertainer, and the top blues and jazz artists were eager to perform with her. But within just a few years, Bessie's life and career would take a dramatic downturn.

The Jazz Blues

Jazz and the blues are different styles of music, but they are like first cousins. Both musical styles developed in the southern United States and both have roots tracing back to traditional western African songs. While they may be related, they are distinct musical styles.

Jazz originated in New Orleans, evolving from the Crescent City's brass band musical culture. These bands played everything from funeral hymns to parades. The bands gradually worked their way to local bars and dance halls, where jazz developed. Jazz was identified by piano and horns, including the saxophone, the trombone, and the cornet. It was also heavily influenced by ragtime music. The blues were born in the Mississippi Delta and were usually played by a solo act, accompanied by a slide guitar.

Jazz quickly blossomed from a regional style into a national craze. Mainstream radio play helped spread its popularity. Also, jazz

was not viewed as African-American music; it was marketed to blacks and whites equally. By contrast, blues music was heavily identified with the southern African-American culture, so its popularity took longer to cross over to mainstream America.

Jazz is primarily an instrumental style, while blues is defined by its vocals.

Perhaps the biggest distinction is that the blues tend to reflect the life experiences of everyday working people. Many songs talk about personal or political issues that impact the daily lives of people. Overall, jazz is more upbeat and doesn't express social attitudes; it's more about the melodies.

NEW ORLEANS JAZZ & HERITAGE FESTIVAL

PRESENTED BY

Chapter 4

The Depression Blues

In 1929, Jack came up with an idea for a new show he would call Steamboat Days. Bessie liked the idea and gave him three thousand dollars to start production while she was on tour. Instead, Jack used the money to produce a show for a blues singer with whom he was having an affair. When Bessie read about the show while on tour in Cincinnati, for once she was not irate. This time, she broke down and cried. Jack's latest betrayal effectively ended the marriage, but while the relationship was over, neither Bessie nor Jack ever filed for divorce.

In June of 1929, Bessie was hired to appear in a short film called *St. Louis Blues* based on her hit song of the same name. The song's composers, Kenneth Adams and W.C. Handy, wrote the script, which was about a love triangle. In the film, Bessie catches her boyfriend with another woman. After he breaks up with her, Bessie sings "St. Louis Blues" while leaning against a bar, a glass of whisky nearby. This was Bessie's only film appearance, and the only known footage of her singing.

The short was a success, but Bessie didn't have much time to bask in her accomplishment. Angry at her decision to leave the marriage, Jack kidnapped their son from Bessie's Philadelphia home and filed neglect and endangerment charges against Bessie with the Society for the Prevention of Cruelty to Children (SPCC). The courts made Viola Jack Jr.'s temporary guardian. Later they sent Jack Jr. to live with his biological father. It would be years before he would come back to live with Bessie.

In May 1929, Bessie appeared in the Broadway show *Pansy*. Although she received positive reviews, the show bombed and closed after just three performances. While Bessie had her music to fall back on, it was clear her star was starting to fade. Talking films were rapidly growing in popularity, as was radio, so vaudeville started to fall out of favor. But the biggest blow to her career was the stock market crash in October 1929 that signaled the start of the Great Depression.

Almost immediately, record sales declined. TOBA canceled shows as more and more vaudeville theaters closed. When TOBA went out of business, Bessie had to book her own shows. While she was still able to put together a tour, she could not command the same salary she had just a year or two earlier. She had to sell her railcar and cut down on her lavish lifestyle to make ends meet.

In July 1930, Bessie recorded "Black Mountain Blues." Columbia, which was struggling financially, produced only around 2,000 copies. In November of the following year, Bessie recorded her last two songs for Columbia: "Safety Mama" and "Need a Little Sugar in My Bowl." After recording 160 songs and selling hundreds of thousands of records over nine years, Bessie's contract was canceled in 1931.

Now, she only had touring to support her. While in Chicago in 1930, she had met up with an old friend named Richard Morgan, who was a bootlegger. They began a romantic relationship. Morgan was very patient and did not get upset with Bessie's drinking or her rowdy behavior.

In 1933, producer John Hammond invited Bessie to New York to record songs for his Okeh label, paying her $150 for four recordings. On these recordings, Bessie's style incorporates elements of swing—an effort to keep up with the musical times.

As the 1930s progressed, it became harder for Bessie to book shows in the larger Northern and Midwestern cities, but she continued to be popular throughout the small towns of the South, the same places where she first performed in traveling shows. After several lean years, things started looking up again. Bessie seemed poised for a comeback—until tragedy struck.

During his 54-year career at Columbia Records, John Hammond discovered some of the greatest musical acts of the twentieth century, including Billie Holiday, Count Basie, Benny Goodman, Aretha Franklin, Bob Dylan, and Bruce Springsteen.

Hammond was born in 1910 to an important New York family. He grew up in a six-story mansion in New York City, but he was drawn to the jazz and blues music he heard played by the household staff. He enjoyed hanging out at Harlem's Alhambra Theater and Roseland Ballroom, where top blues singers performed.

After leaving Yale University in 1931, John wrote jazz columns for *Gramophone* and *Melody Maker.* He used his trust fund money to promote the recordings of black artists, and he staged jazz concerts at the Manhattan theater he bought, hiring racially mixed bands.

In his memoirs, he noted, "I heard no color line in the music . . . To bring recognition to the Negro's supremacy in jazz was the most effective and constructive form of social protest I could think of."[1]

In 1933, Hammond became the recording representative for the British branch of Columbia Records. He asked a then unknown clarinetist named Benny Goodman to recruit musicians from Harlem for a recording session with Bessie Smith. A year later he supervised the first recordings of Billie Holiday.

Hammond had a knack for sensing what the next musical trend would be.

His last major signing was Texas blues guitarist Stevie Ray Vaughan in 1983. Hammond was inducted into the Rock and Roll Hall of Fame in 1986. He died a year later from complications following a stroke.

Count Basie (piano),
Benny Goodman (clarinet),
Bessie Smith (back), and
Billie Holiday

Chapter 5

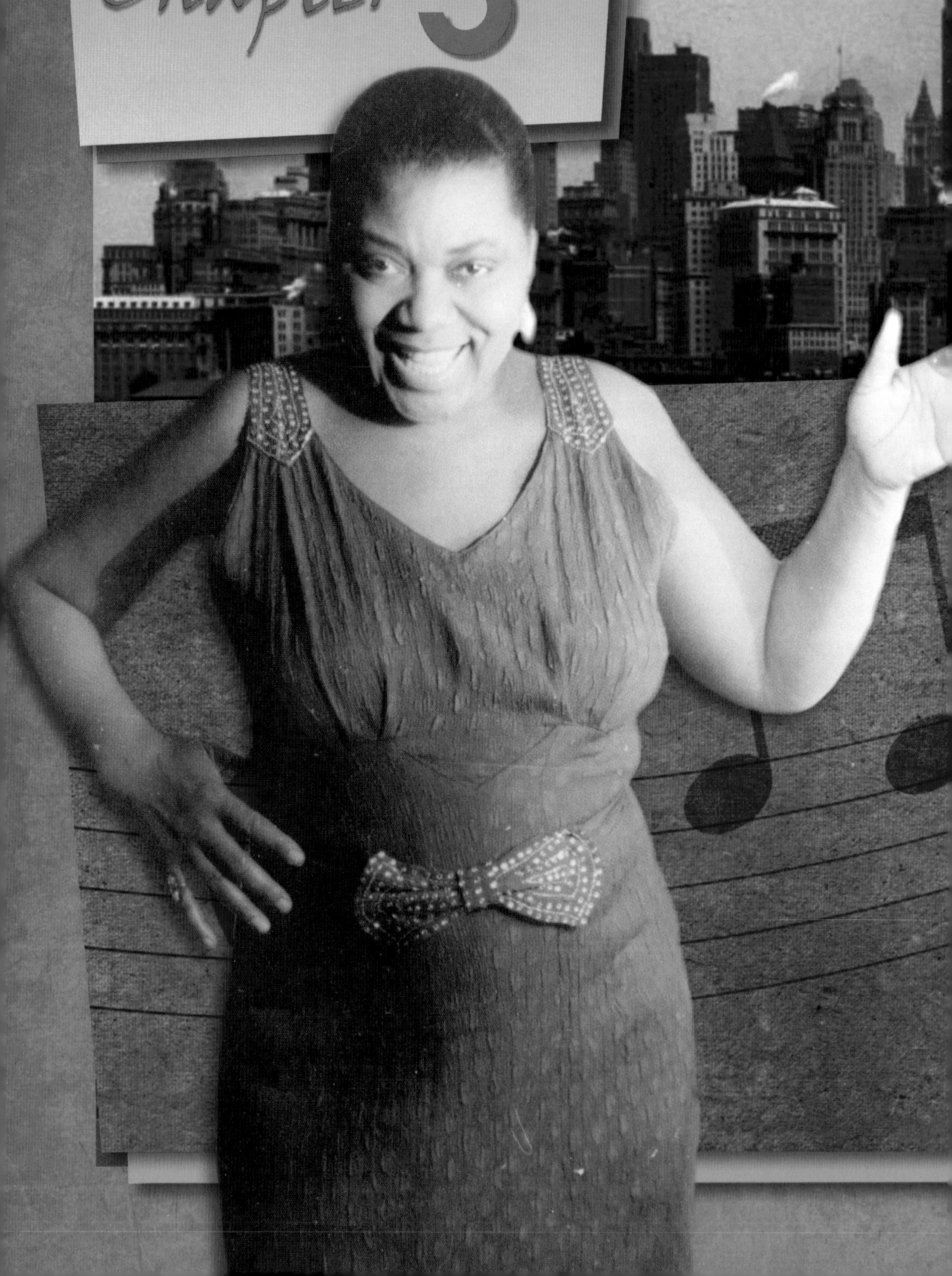

The Death of Bessie Smith

She may not have been a big star in the general public's eyes, but within the blues community, Bessie Smith was still considered one of the best singers around. She was still in demand, even if the number of tour dates continued to shrink. In 1935 she played at the Apollo Theater, and a year later temporarily filled in for an ailing Billie Holiday in *Stars Over Broadway*. In 1936, she was invited to appear at a Sunday afternoon concert at Manhattan's Famous Door club on 52nd Street. Then in the summer of 1937, Columbia executive John Hammond asked Bessie to participate in his "From Spirituals to Swing" concert, an event some saw as further proof that her career was making a comeback. It would feature more than forty jazz performers, including Meade "Lux" Lewis, Count Basie, Big Joe Turner, Sonny Terry, and Helen Humes. Hammond also later revealed that he was arranging a recording session with Bessie and Count Basie's band.

The recording industry had found a new golden goose in swing music, which Bessie had started incorporating into her act. Plus, the blues was regaining its past popularity. It seemed the lean years were about to be behind her. And with her relationship with Richard Morgan solid and secure, Bessie's personal and professional lives seemed on solid ground.

On September 26, 1937, Bessie performed in Memphis, Tennessee. After the show Richard—now acting as her manager—packed the car

In the 1930s, Bessie's career slumped, partly because of the economic woes brought on by the Great Depression and partly because the popularity of the blues diminished as jazz and swing grew increasingly popular. Bessie adjusted her act and by 1937 was on the road to a comeback.

and they headed south to Darling, Mississippi, for her next show. While driving along Route 61, near Clarksdale, Mississippi, Richard suddenly came up on a slow-moving truck. He tried swerving around the truck but misjudged the distance. He rear-ended the truck at high speed. Bessie was in the passenger's seat, and it is believed she had her arm resting on the sill of the window. The truck's tailgate sheared off the roof of the car and severed her arm at the elbow. Richard was unharmed.

One of the first people on the scene was Dr. Hugh Smith and his friend Henry Broughton, on their way to a fishing trip. Dr. Smith examined Bessie as she lay on the road. The right side of her body had been crushed, and she was losing a lot of blood from her arm injury. He applied a tourniquet to her arm using a handkerchief while Broughton went to a nearby house to call an ambulance.

Bessie was admitted to Clarksdale's Afro-American Hospital, where surgeons amputated her right arm. She died later that morning without regaining consciousness. A story later circulated that she died after being refused admittance to a whites-only hospital, but that was proven to be a false rumor.

Bessie's body was taken back to Philadelphia, where thousands of mourners showed up to pay their respects as they filed past her gold-trimmed, velvet-lined casket. Bessie's biographer described the scene:

On Monday, October 4, 1937, Philadelphia witnessed one of the most spectacular funerals in its history. Bessie Smith, a black superstar of the previous decade—a 'has been,' fatally injured on a dark Mississippi road eight days earlier—was given a send-off befitting the star she had never really ceased to be . . . When word of her death reached the black community, the body had to be moved [to another location] which more readily accommodated the estimated ten thousand admirers who filed past her bier on Sunday, October 3. The crowd outside was now seven thousand strong, and policemen were having a hard time holding it back. To those who had known Bessie in her better days, the sight was familiar.[1]

This mural located in Clarksdale, Mississippi, depicts Bessie performing

Although Bessie was known for her powerful singing voice, she was also a talented dancer.

Despite her personal problems, Bessie Smith remained an exciting performer who influenced performers in the generations that followed. In 2011, Miche Braden played Bessie in the off-Broadway production of *The Devil's Music: The Life and Blues of Bessie Smith*.

She was buried at Mount Lawn Cemetery in Sharon Hill, Pennsylvania. For more than 35 years, her grave did not have a headstone. Finally, in 1970, singer Janis Joplin and the North Philadelphia chapter of the NAACP bought the singer a proper marker. The epitaph they chose reads: The Greatest Blues Singer in the World Will Never Stop Singing.

Clarksdale, Mississippi

It is somewhat fitting that Bessie Smith died in Clarksdale. Most music historians consider Clarksdale ground zero for the blues. Although it only has 20,000 residents, Clarksdale's homegrown talent reads like a Who's Who: Muddy Waters, Ike Turner, and Sam Cooke all lived in the area. Most famously, though, its pedigree evolved from legendary bluesman Robert Johnson.

According to legend, it was at the crossroads in Clarksdale—at Routes 61 and 49—where Johnson sold his soul to the devil in exchange for extraordinary talent on the guitar. His musical ability seemed to improve overnight, and his career took off. Some of his more enduring songs are "Cross Road Blues" and "Me and the Devil Blues," whose lyrics keep the legend alive.

Johnson, however, did not get to enjoy his talents for very long. The devil, it is said, took his due when Johnson died painfully, probably from poisoning, at the age of twenty-seven.

Actor Morgan Freeman is co-owner of a blues club in Clarksdale called Ground Zero. He says locals still like to believe the devil showed up in their town. He told the *Chicago Tribune* in 2001, "You have the devil, and everybody sort of accepts that he is the [bringer] of bad times. And the blues is an expression of that. It's letting it out, the way you vent. If I didn't have bad luck, I'd have no luck at all—that's the blues."[2]

1894 Bessie Smith is born in Chattanooga, Tennessee, on April 15 to Laura (maiden name Owens) and William Smith.

1903 By her birthday, Bessie has lost her father, mother, and two of her brothers.

1904 Bessie's oldest brother, Clarence, leaves home to join a small traveling troupe owned by Moses Stokes.

1911 Bessie meets tap dancer Wayne "Buzzin" Burton in Alabama.

1912 Lonnie and Cora Fisher, managers of the Moses Stokes' Traveling Show, give Bessie an audition; she signs with them as a dancer and meets blues singer Ma Rainey.

1915 Bessie joins Rainey as a performer with Pat Chappelle's Rabbit's Foot Minstrels.

1918 Forms the Liberty Belles Revue in Atlanta, Georgia.

1920 Marries Earl Love, who dies before 1922.

1923 In Philadelphia, Bessie marries Jack Gee on June 7, just as her first record is released. Her "Down-hearted Blues" is the first "race record" issued by Columbia, and becomes a smash hit.

1926 Bessie and Jack adopt Jack Jr.

1929 Bessie learns of Jack's affair with another singer and ends their marriage, although the two never seek a divorce. She appears in the Broadway flop *Pansy* and in the movie *St. Louis Blues*.

1933 At the suggestion of John Hammond, she records four sides for Okeh, earning $37.50 per selection.

1937 On September 26, Bessie and boyfriend Richard Morgan are in a car accident; Bessie is critically injured and dies the next morning. Her funeral is held in Philadelphia on October 4.

1938 On December 23, John Hammond presents his concert From Spirituals to Swing in Carnegie Hall; it is dedicated to Bessie, who was to have performed in it.

1948 J.D. Salinger writes the short story "Blue Melody," originally titled "Scratchy Needle on a Phonograph Record," which is inspired by the life of Bessie Smith.

1959 Edward Albee writes a one-act play called *The Death of Bessie Smith*.

1970 Singer Janis Joplin and the daughter of Bessie's former housekeeper, Juanita Green, buy a tombstone to mark Bessie's grave.

1989 Bessie is inducted to the Rock and Roll Hall of Fame.

1923

"My Sweetie Went Away (She Didn't Say Where, When Or Why)"
"Down-hearted Blues"
"Gulf Coast Blues"
"Baby Won't You Please Come Home"
"Oh Daddy Blues"
"Keeps On A Rainin' (Papa, He Can't Make No Time)"
" 'Tain't Nobody's Bizness If I Do"
"Mamas Got The Blues"
"Outside of That"
"Bleeding Hearted Blues"
"Lady Luck Blues"
"Yodling Blues"
"Midnight Blues"
"If You Don't Know Who Will?"
"Nobody In Town Can Bake A Sweet Jelly Roll Like Mine"
"Jail-House Blues"
"Sam Jones Blues"
"St. Louis Gal"
"Cemetery Blues"
"Graveyard Dream Blues"
"Far Away Blues"
"I'm Going Back To My Used To Be"
"Any Woman's Blues"
"Chicago Bound Blues"
"Mistreatin' Daddy"

1924

"Frosty Morining Blues
"Evesdropper's Blues"
"Haunted House Blues"
"Easy Come Easy Go Blues"
"Pinchbacks—Take 'Em Away"
"Rocking Chair Blues"
"Sorrowful Blues"
"Ticket Agent Ease Your Window Down"
"Bowevil Blues"
"Frankie Blues"
"Hateful Blues"
"Moonshine Blues"
"Lou'siana Low Down Blues"
"Mountaintop Blues"
"House Rent Blues"

"Work House Blues"
"Salt Water Blues"
"Rainy Weather Blues"
"The Bye Bye Blues"
"Weeping Willow Blues"
"Sing Sing Prison Blues"
"Follow The Deal On Down"
"Sinful Blues"
"Love Me Daddy Blues"
"Woman's Trouble Blues"
"Dying Gambler's Blues"

1925
"Cold In Hand Blues"
"Reckless Blues"
"Sobbin' Hearted Blues"
"St. Louis Blues"
"You've Been A Good Old Wagon"
"Squeeze Me"
"Them 'Has Been' Blues"
"Soft Pedal Blues"
"Dixie Flyer Blues"
"Careless Love Blues"
"Nashville Woman's Blues"
"I Aint' Goin' To Play No Second Fiddle"
"J.C. Holmes Blues"
"He's Gone Blues"
"I Ain't Got Nobody"
"Nobody's Blues But Mine'
"My Man Blues"
"Florida Bound Blues"
"New Gulf Coast Blues"
"At The Christmas Ball"
"I've Been Mistreated And I Don't Like It"
"Golden Rule Blues"
"Red Mountain Blues"
"Lonesome Desert Blues"
"I Want Ev'ry Bit Of It"
"What's The Matter Now?"

1926
"Jazzbo Brown From Memphis Town"
"The Gin House Blues"

"Baby Doll"
"Hard Driving Papa"
"Lost Your Head Blues"
"Money Blues"
"Hard Time Blues"
"Honey Man Blues"
"One And Two Blues"
"Young Woman's Blues"
"Sweet Mistreater"
"Back-Water Blues"

1927

"Preachin' The Blues"
"After You've Gone"
"Muddy Water (A Mississippi Moan)"
"Lock And Key"
"A Good Man Is Hard To Find"
"Mean Old Bed Bug Blues"
"There'll Be A Hot Time In The Old Town To-Night"
"Homeless Blues"
"Hot Spring's Blues"
"Looking For My Man Blues"
"Send Me To The 'Lectric Chair"
"Dyin' By The Hour"
"Them's Graveyard Words"
"Foolish Man Blues"
"Trombone Cholly"
"I Used To Be Your Sweet Mama"
"Pickpocket Blues"
"Thinking Blues"
"I'd Rather Be Dead And Buried In My Grave"
"It Won't Be You"
"Standin' In The Rain Blues"
"Spider Man Blues"
"Empty Bed Blues (Part 1)"

1928

"Empty Bed Blues (Part 2)"
"Put It Right Here"
"(Or Keep It Out Of There)"
"Devil's Gonna Git You"
"Poorman's Blues"
"Slow And Easy Man"

"Washwoman's Blues"
"Yes Indeed He Do!"
"You Ought To Ashamed"
"Me And My Gin"
"Please Help Me Get Him Off My Mind"
"I'm Wild About That Thing"
"Kitchen Man"
"You've Got To Get Me Some"
"I Got What It Takes (But It Breaks My Heart To Give It Away)"
"I've Got What It Takes"
"Nobody Knows You When You're Down And Out"
"Take It Right Back ('Cause I Don't Want It Here)"
"He's Got Me Goin'"

1929
"It Makes My Love Come Down"
"Dirty No-Gooder's Blues"
"Wasted Life Blues"
"Blue Spirit Blues"
"Don't Cry Baby"
"Worn Out Papa"
"You Don't Understand"
"Keep It To Yourself"
"New Orleans Hop Scop Blues"
"Baby Have Pity On Me"
"See If I Care"
"Moan Mourners"
"On Revival Day"
"(A Rhythmic Spiritual)"
"Black Mountain Blues"
"Hustlin' Dan"

1930
"Blue Blues"
"In The House Blues"
"Long Old Road"
"Shipwreck Blues"
"Need A Little Sugar In My Bowl"

1933
"Gimme a Pigfoot"
"Do Your Duty"

Chapter 1 Klan Encounter

1. Roy Rosenzweig Center for History and New Media, *The Birth of a Nation and Black Protest,* http://chnm.gmu.edu/episodes/the-birth-of-a-nation-and-black-protest/
2. Chris Albertson, *Bessie* (New Haven, CT: Yale University Press, 1972), pp. 132–133.

Chapter 2 Born to Perform

1. Dan Morgenstern, *Jazz People* (Cambridge, MA: Da Capo Press, 1993); quoting from N. Shapiro and N. Hentoff, eds., *Hear Me Talkin' to Ya* (New York: Rinehart, 1955), pp. 243, 249–251.

Chapter 3 Empress of the Blues

1. Günther Schuller, *Early Jazz* (New York: Oxford University Press, 1986), p. 229.

Chapter 4 The Depression Blues

1. John Hammond, *John Hammond on Record: An Autobiography* (New York: Ridge Press, 1977), p. 68.

Chapter 5 The Death of Bessie Smith

1. Chris Albertson, *Bessie* (New Haven, CT: Yale University Press, 1972), p. 1.
2. Robert K. Elder, *Chicago Tribune,* "Morgan Freeman's Web: 'Spider' Just the Latest in a Long Line of Movies and Music Projects," April 7, 2001, http://articles.chicagotribune.com/2001-04-07/news/0104070188_1_spider-love-scene-alex-cross/2

BOOKS

Manera, Alexandria. *Bessie Smith*. Chicago: Raintree, 2003.

Myers, Walter Dean, and Christopher Myers (Illustrator). *Jazz*. New York: Holiday House, 2008.

Patrick, James. *Robert Johnson: Legend of the Delta Blues*. New York: Gareth Stevens Publishing, 2010.

Stauffacher, Sue. *Bessie Smith and the Night Riders*. New York: Putnam Juvenile, 2006.

WORKS CONSULTED

Albertson, Chris. *Bessie*. New Haven, CT: Yale University Press, 1972.

Braziel, Jana Evans. " 'Bye, Bye, Baby': Race, Bisexuality, and the Blues in the Music of Bessie Smith and Janis Joplin." *Popular Music and Society,* 27 (2004): 3–22.

Davis, Angela Y. *Blues Legacies and Black Feminism*. New York: Pantheon Books, 1998.

Elder, Robert K. "Morgan Freeman's Web: 'Spider' Just the Latest in a Long Line of Movies and Music Projects." *Chicago Tribune,* April 7, 2001. http://articles.chicagotribune.com/2001-04-07/news/0104070188_1_spider-love-scene-alex-cross/2

Feinstein, Elaine. *Bessie Smith: Empress of the Blues*. New York: Penguin Books, 1985.

Hammond, John. *John Hammond on Record: An Autobiography*. New York: Ridge Press, 1977.

Marks, Carole, and Diana Edkins. *Style Makers and Rule Breakers of the Harlem Renaissance*. New York: Crown, 1999.

Morgenstern, Dan. *Jazz People*. Cambridge, MA: Da Capo Press, 1993.

Roy Rosenzweig Center for History and New Media. *The Birth of a Nation and Black Protest*. http://chnm.gmu.edu/episodes/the-birth-of-a-nation-and-black-protest/

Schuller, Günther. *Early Jazz*. New York: Oxford University Press, 1986.

Scott, Michelle R. *Blues Empress in Black Chattanooga: Bessie Smith and the Emerging Urban South*. Champagne, IL: University of Illinois Press, 2008.

ON THE INTERNET

Jazz at the Smithsonian Institution
http://www.smithsonianjazz.org/

The Minnesota Blues Society, "Blues for Kids"
http://www.mnbs.org/bfk.html

The Mississippi Blues Trail
http://www.msbluestrail.org/index.aspx

PBS, Jazz Biography: "Bessie Smith"
http://www.pbs.org/jazz/biography/artist_id_smith_bessie.htm

PBS Kids, Jazz
http://pbskids.org/jazz/

PBS: The Blues
http://www.pbs.org/theblues/

PHOTO CREDITS: Cover—Joe Rasemas; pp. 4, 16, 24, 30—Library of Congress; p. 8—D.W. Griffith; p. 12—Digital Library of Georgia; pp. 10, 15, 35—Frank Driggs Collection/Getty Images; pp. 20, 26—Michael Ochs Archives/Getty Images; p. 32—Gilles Petard/Redferns/Getty Images; p. 36—AP Photo/David Gertsen & Associates/John Quilty. Every effort has been made to locate all copyright holders of material used in this book. If any errors or omissions have occurred, corrections will be made in future editions of the book.

bootlegger (BOOT-lay-gur)—Someone who makes and/or sells alcohol illegally.

boycott (BOY-kot)—To avoid buying something in order to make a political point.

Deep South—Parts of the United States that have or had strong feelings about states' rights: Alabama, Georgia, Louisiana, Mississippi, and South Carolina.

diction (DIK-shun)—Choice of words and how clearly they are expressed.

epitaph (EH-pih-taf)—A saying on a tombstone.

hypnotism (HIP-noh-tism)—Causing a sleeplike trance.

intimidated (in-TIH-mih-day-ted)—Made to feel frightened of someone or something.

intonation (in-toh-NAY-shin)—The playing of notes in tune; the ability to achieve exact tones in music.

microtonal—In music, involving tones smaller than a half-tone.

minstrel (MIN-strul)—A traveling entertainer who sings, recites poetry, performs skits, and dances.

Negro (NEE-groh)—An African American. This term, which means "black," was often used in the early 1900s, but it is now considered impolite.

poverty (PAH-ver-tee)—Extreme lack; lacking the socially acceptable amount of wealth.

Reconstruction (ree-kun-STRUK-shun)—The policies of rebuilding and restructuring the South following the Civil War.

segregation (seh-greh-GAY-shun)—A legal policy of separating the races.

sharecropper (SHAYR-krah-per)—A farmer who grows crops on someone else's land and receives a share of the profit as payment.

tenement (TEN-eh-ment)—A run-down and overcrowded apartment complex.

trust fund—A bank account set up by one person to be used by another person.

white supremacy (WYT suh-PREH-muh-see)—The belief that white people are better than people of other races.

About the Author

Entertainment journalist and children's book author Kathleen Tracy specializes in celebrity biographies. An avid sports fan, she lives in Southern California with her two dogs and African gray parrot.